# HOW TO BE HAPPY THOUGH HUMAN

T0151887

ALSO BY KATE CAMP

*Unfamiliar Legends of the Stars* (1998)
*Realia* (2001)
*Beauty Sleep* (2005)
*The Mirror of Simple Annihilated Souls* (2010)
*Snow White's Coffin* (2013)
*The Internet of Things* (2017)

# HOW TO BE HAPPY
# THOUGH HUMAN

## New and Selected Poems

## Kate Camp

ANANSI

Published in Canada in 2020 and the USA in 2020 by House of Anansi Press Inc.
www.houseofanansi.com

24  23  22  21  20     1  2  3  4  5

Library and Archives Canada Cataloguing in Publication

Title: How to be happy though human : new and selected poems / Kate Camp.
Other titles: Poems. Selections
Names: Camp, Kate, author.
Identifiers: Canadiana (print) 20200206125 | Canadiana (ebook) 20200206133 |
ISBN 9781487008376 (softcover) | ISBN 9781487009076 (Kindle) |
ISBN 9781487008383 (EPUB)
Classification: LCC PR9639.3.C35 A6 2020 | DDC 821/.92—dc23

Cover design: Alysia Shewchuk
Cover image: *Winter store of apples at 'Cheslyn Rise,' July 1908*, by Leslie Adkin.
Gift of G. L. Adkin family estate, 1964. Te Papa.

*We acknowledge for their financial support of our publishing program the Canada Council for the Arts, the Ontario Arts Council, and the Government of Canada.*

Printed and bound in Canada

For my mother, Elaine Lynskey

# CONTENTS

from *The Internet of Things* (2017)

Life has become complicated. Work is hard, and play is not easy. Thought is often painful, and even love has for many become a torment rather than a joy. The author, a well-known psychologist, explains in this stimulating book how the delicate human machine may be kept smoothly running, by adapting one's own psychological equipment to one's own needs. In the course of his discussion he touches helpfully on nearly every important problem of everyday life.

—W. Beran Wolfe, M.D., *How to Be Happy Though Human* (1931)


Nothing has changed.
Except the run of rivers,
the shapes of forests, shores, deserts and glaciers.
The little soul roams among those landscapes,
disappears, returns, draws near, moves away,
evasive and a stranger to itself,
now sure, now uncertain of its own existence,
whereas the body is and is and is
and has nowhere to go.

—Wisława Szymborska, 'Tortures' (1986)

# INTRODUCTION

It was my good luck to meet Kate Camp at an event we both participated in at the New Zealand International Arts Festival in March 2010. It was my first reading outside North America and I was both grateful and very nervous. Kate struck me as funny, unpretentious, tall, and comfortable in her own skin. The poems she read made perfect sense to me; apart from the accent, she could easily be taken for an established talent from Vancouver or upstate New York. I flew home with the book she launched that spring, *The Mirror of Simple Annihilated Souls*. I was so taken with it I wrote an essay to run alongside two of Camp's poems in the fall issue of the Toronto literary journal *Brick*.

Fast forward three years. A package arrives: a copy of *Snow White's Coffin*, Camp's new collection. I put it on the reading list for my graduate poetry workshop. To my delight, the book also resonated with my student poets. How was it, we wondered, that this poet was largely unknown in Canada and in the US?

To date, the chances of a New Zealand poet publishing a book in Canada are about the same as a Canadian being published in New Zealand – something very close to zero. But when I became poetry editor at Anansi, I knew I was joining a press with a history of publishing international poets. The most recent example, now, is *How to Be Happy Though Human*, published simultaneously by House of Anansi Press in North America and Victoria University of Wellington Press in New Zealand.

Okay, how, then, might we situate Camp's poems next to those of current North American poets? She has a little of Karen Solie's bemused melancholy. She shares Mary Ruefle's humility and philosophical bent. I once thought no one but Ruefle could write a poem like her 'How I Became Impossible'. It now reminds me a little of Camp, especially in the way it moves from amusement to complication to heartbreak at the very end. Camp's books would sit comfortably on a shelf between Kay Ryan and

Brenda Shaughnessy. And though she's not as committed a jokester, Camp also has the offhand humour and recklessness of an early Dean Young. She's funny but never without purpose – but that's not unusual for poets of her generation.

People are born every day. It stands to reason a small number of them will write poetry and an even smaller number of those people will write it well. Still, Camp was born in 1972, which means she's spent all of her adult life in the age of internet. The pertinence of that fact varies with each person, but the internet's revolution of access: to knowledge and disinformation, to art and cultural debris, not to mention its tendency to render notions of high and low culture meaningless – that's liable to colour the way someone sees the world. By contrast, I don't just remember a time before the internet; I had completed my undergraduate degree and most of grad school before I owned a computer.

There are exceptions, but poets born in the 1970s tend to employ a wider range of human emotion in their work than poets born mid-century, for example. More specifically, they allow irony and humour a more prominent role than recently seen in so-called serious poetry. Humour is presence, humour is surprise, and as we can see in several of these poems, it can quickly pivot toward the political.

Another characteristic of poets of this generation is an attraction to plunder and repurposed language. You'll notice the titles of Camp's books all originally meant something else. 'Snow White's coffin' is the nickname given to a particularly well-designed German portable turntable from the mid-1950s; 'the internet of things' is digital jargon; while the book you're holding shares its title with a 1931 self-help volume by W. Beran Wolfe, M.D., a disciple of Alfred Adler.

I tend to imprint on the first book I read by poets I like. For me it was *The Mirror* . . . , whose title sequence (included here) proves that in the right hands redaction and plunder can result in something mesmerising and transformative. Camp is a stylist with great range and an ear for the found poem. But her default mode is a species of collage, a verbal transcript of an immediate interplay among voice, image, and idea.

'I'm an atheist,' Camp said in a 2015 interview, 'but it seems to me utterly incredible that, in this complex world and our complex lives, in any hour, enough things are passing through our consciousness to fill a library.' Camp's aesthetic is not about distilling experience, hers is a poetry of plenty – she's not interested in leaving things out.

No surprise then to find out her writer's notebook is less journal than scrapbook, each thought or line, whether written on a Post-it, bus ticket or stray scrap of paper, dropped between the covers in an effort to preserve the moment it arrived.

I recently asked a poet friend if he felt, as I was starting to, that all poets might be phenomenologists. He paused. 'Yeah, that makes sense. We're more interested in feelings and perceptions than in what things actually are.' But just as there are good poets and better poets there are more rigorous phenomenologists. Exhibit A, from Camp's 'Double Glazing':

This is what light will do:

Slowly take away the room
destroy its layers, its unexpected angles

its demonstrations of the laws of light and how light falls
and how the eye performs its tasks of understanding.

And so, when day is fully here, the window will be empty
that dolls' house theatre, that gold confusion
gone. There will only be the so-called outside world
going about its business made of sound.

Or consider these lines that end her psalm-like 'The Night Sky on Any Day in History':

You could spend your time watching trains
pull their strings of yellow windows along in lines.

Or you might come here, where I am
where I stand upon the rarely silent floor
looking up at the rectangle moon
of our neighbour's window.

Keats spoke of that faculty, handy to all artists, to entertain without undue worry two apparently contradictory concepts simultaneously. Camp has that in spades. Her poems deliberately conflate the inner with the outer, the imagined and the actual, and refuse to concede a divide between the human and the natural. In Camp's poetry it's not quite right to call such concepts 'blurred', it's more that they're contiguous in a fluid and constantly refreshed way of being.

After all, humans share 99% of our DNA with the great apes. A construction site is an anthill when viewed from sufficient height. Looking at the movements of a crowd at a rock concert (remember those?), what doesn't remind you of a murmuration of starlings?

It's not spoiling anything to notice recurring obsessions, going back to Camp's earliest poems. Eyes are important, as are clocks and boyfriends, trains and windows and 'working ports'. Then there's the incendiary beauty of the natural world, ever poised to assert itself. Anyone who's been to the antipodes knows that if it isn't all about the birds it's at least mostly all about the birds. These poems are episodically obsessed with them: parrots, magpies and escaped budgies; swans and their paddleboat facsimiles; news hawkers cawing at train stations; terns, gulls, more gulls, and the gulls 'that came to the park in anticipation of a storm at sea'.

For those of us living this side of the equator lucky enough to have stumbled on Kate Camp's poetry, *How to Be Happy Though Human* collects key poems from six books – plus a substantial sample of new work – in one volume.

As for the rest, you're in for a treat.

*Kevin Connolly, Toronto, June 2020*

# HOW TO BE HAPPY THOUGH HUMAN

# HALLELUJAH

Summer rain at the beach house.
I couldn't sleep – not the rain which was gentle
but percussion of water in the downpipe.

Making tea by the light of the street lamp
I was singing *Hallelujah*
I never remember the verses
the roof and the chair and the tongue
but I can fill those parts in with sounds
in the back of my throat
like the sounds you make to animals.

As I stepped on the pedal of the rubbish bin
the grey mouth opened and there
among the onion skins and tea bags
piled like tiny sacks of wheat
was a *multicoloured flashing disco candle*
which I'd thrown out earlier
while testing the *24pcs for ten dollars*.

I preserve myself at that moment:
coloured light playing on my face from below
teabag held on a spoon, an offering
a medicine, my foot on the pedal, braking
accelerating, making loud or quiet
and the dead Leonard Cohen
all around me in the orange streetlight
and the rain, as soft as water

and you
asleep in the next room
thin and pale
as the body of Christ

while I experienced a miracle
all by myself.

# PANIC BUTTON

Tusiata tells me that the Bedouin
hardly drink any water.
*They bury onions in the desert*
she says, though I'm not sure
if the two are connected.

So many things can go wrong
inside a human life, it's almost comical.
You find yourself in a house,
in a night, with everyone you love
breathing in and out somewhere
and if you thought about it properly
you'd just throw up in terror.

Instead I have this button in my pocket
not like a panic button, just a button
that's come loose, and it fits
into the curve of my thumb and finger
as I turn it over and over.
I keep it in my pocket
like you keep a pebble in your mouth
in the desert, to make saliva flow.

## GULLS

In Homer, the gods
take the place of consciousness.

For me, it is birds.
Grey gulls

seen from above,
a tan and white pigeon

bringing amoral intelligence
to the balcony wall.

Geoff says they are really getting tough on birds
in Brighton. Bringing in a bylaw.

I remember his balcony
it's really just the roof of the room downstairs

but when you climb out the window
you get a view of the sea

and the ferris wheel
which I believe is gone, or going

it was an eyesore
all the locals said

though I – of course –
thought it was wonderful

and the burned down pier
out in the water.

# GULLS AGAIN

When I've been where gulls are
I've always been at ground level

the glassy sand and its clouds
my memory of the sunken poles

that used to run along the river there
(the creek / the stream )

with occasional strands of wire.
Gulls still go around in pairs

meowing like cats
appear disgruntled when seen on foot

a faintly urban irascibility to this one
as it gathers moss from a scenic grave.

The ones in Brighton, Geoff says
are three times the size

and nothing at all to do with the souls of sailors.
I go back to pretending

the coos of pigeons
are the howls of far distant wolf packs

and that I am an Arctic explorer
who when I turn to my window

sees nothing but herself
and a dark herringbone of forest.

# THE LAW OF EXPRESSED EMOTION

The law is, that those who love you
will not help you get better.

Yes, they will sit next to you in a car
and take you through space

both moving forward at exactly the same speed
showing your profiles to each other

which are ageing rather more cruelly
than the fronts of you.

They will do things like park their car on the footpath for you
leaving only a card on the dashboard as a plea for clemency

and they will do explaining for you
when people do not understand your language

because you appear absolutely fluent while in fact
you are somewhat on fire.

They might take you to the monastery
with its not very important frescoes of Jesus

faintly visible and let you look down into valleys
that literally never see the sun.

They hope you will find this soothing
but perhaps it will be terrifying, the train of marvels

with its gorges and viaducts
and the medieval villages it passes though

on its way to the coast.
Maybe better to take you to the wardrobe

the *armoire*, where all the sheets and towels are
and where there used to be stickers of the Incredible Hulk

which glowed in the dark.
Except we gave the wardrobe away

left it out on the street with a sign saying
FREE

and when we woke up
or when we looked around

it was gone.

# HERE'S THE THING

Just as my mother – as a woman younger than I am now
with black hair unlike anyone else in the family –
would take the leather-encased Sanyo to the washing line
so I go to the line with my phone in the strap of my bra
and I listen to voices say *here's the thing*.
I got my love of American politics from her,
born into her fear that she would die
before the end of Watergate.

I open and close the jaws of various pegs – the good ones
and the weak, old ones that sometimes snap apart
because it seems plastic can decay
though not, obviously, enough or in the right way.

\*

We went there, to the Watergate Hotel.
In its basement a strange mini mart, disreputable hair salon
the kind of amazed-they're-in-business shops
you see in small towns and suburbs everywhere.
The room had a view of the Potomac
its autumnal trees and misty colour palette.

Here's the thing: we didn't win the election.
In the morning, when Hillary gave her concession speech,
I moved across to the other bed
so I could cry in Mum's arms.

\*

I put a hook into the wall by the washing line
so the basket can balance on the ledge.
*Did you Michael?* Mum would say,

because my father delights
in such small acts of household order.

Of course I should switch off my phone and just breathe
allow the glistening spheres of rain
on the renga renga, the pink twigs of the eucalpyt
the smell of the glassy air to be enough.
But I can't do a damn thing about time,
can't wish it away, slow it down,
and I like my voices, I like to have my voices with me.

And then, an explosion of gulls
bursts from the sports field to the lowered sky

up! up! up! up! up! up! up!
they seem to cry.

## MY FATHER'S TEETH

A black eye like makeup
purple in the hollow of the nose
and below in an arc, in the pouch of skin,
blue black calligraphy.

You're still bringing out small pieces of bone
finding them on your tongue
like the lizards brought in by my neighbour's cat.
And now they've sunk the screw into your jaw

to which they can attach the tooth
and that will be a little iceberg
made of something from the future
to outlive you, outlive us all.

Your gold tooth, a cap of gold,
fascinated us as children – I never saw another.
It was not piratical more *English* –
which meant more black and white.

It's strange to think we've got our childhood teeth
with us through the eras
our own personal cemetery
hardest substance of the human body

but they can crumble, detonated by some stone
for you it's always overseas
some piece of the world
eaten on an unfamiliar, overpopulated shore.

We look out at the wharves we know.
Clouds of sawdust coming off the stacks of logs.

Tugboats keeping busy, like the charming
self-important little dogs that bring comfort to the old.

That's us, we're the old, or we hold them inside us
in our teeth, with no next crop waiting to push up.
There's only one of everything
one moon, one sun, one dad, one mum.

You come to the door
to watch me drive away.

# EVENING

Shadows in peripheral vision
broken by lines of venetian blinds
the birds that are nesting here, inside the granite slabs
approach their home.

It's difficult to enter
an almost imperceptible void in the sheer face
they flutter toward and fail
once, twice.

Sometimes I have seen one bring a strand of dried grass.

It's usually in the evening I notice them
but that may be my routine not theirs
a time when my mind is moving like a cloud to the outside world.

Soon I will stand, bring my spine to its upright phase,
take my coat from its hook, descend to the carpark
and through the winter evening to my home.

But now I watch
the wedge of a black tail disappearing,
the white lines of shit fanning out below.

I don't want to tell Peter about the birds.
I never mentioned them to Steve, when he was here.

I can't imagine the space they're in
the dark coolness of the back of the stone
but you can make a home
just about anywhere

even in your own hand
when you hold it over your mouth
because you're starting to cry.

# ONE TRAIN MAY HIDE ANOTHER

I had almost forgotten what it is
to look for the numbers of letterboxes
with the weeping foliage of trees overhead
their twisted trunks like enormously magnified
pieces of thread.

And then what it is to come to a gate
and find with a gentle shock
it has no latch and can simply be pushed open
to knock at a glass ribbed door and see a shape approach
approximation of a person and you are there
in the home of a stranger
not sure how many layers of clothing to remove
in the first instance.

There's something I mistake for an artwork
which turns out to be percussion.
And when the band plays
I make a kind of eye contact I very rarely make
to meet the eyes, at eye level, of the tall acquaintance
next to me with a look that openly says
it is good to be alive in this very second.
Not good. *Thrilling.*

Two things are disappearing at the moment.
Trolley bus wires, and orange streetlights.

I walk back up the street with the guitar player
and the banjo player and the man who played percussion
barely balancing on his bicycle behind us.

Guitar says she was ready to hate the new streetlights
but instead finds she loves them

that they somehow show the moisture
by which I think she means a kind of halo.

Then I say about the trolley bus wires
how one day the sound of them
will take us back
like the sound of dial-up internet.

I'm thinking about the sound of the boys
selling papers at the railway station
*Paaaayeee-peeeee-er.* They can't have been wearing flat caps
in the nineteen-eighties but the sound
is near Victorian in its ancientness.

I've got a lot of history in the city.
Double bass I used to run with in my twenties
he taught us to stretch our calves by standing in the gutter.

Violin was out the back of my flat when I was nineteen.
I would put the speakers in the garden
and play 'Be Mine Tonight' again and again
running inside to rewind the tape.
He's shocked to find I am middle aged.
I'm not shocked. Inside me are the Russian dolls
of the women and girls I've been before
each more beautiful and unhappy than the current.

I try to remember nights when I have walked along streets
and can only think of two.
The night I went to dinner in an autumn so windless
that cars were covered in yellow leaves under yellow lights
and the night we walked home that summer

and saw the sign *Un train peut en cacher un autre*:
one train may hide another.

# ORGANS OF SENSE AND VOICE

I have a new minute in my day.
In the shower, once the water stops
I rest my arms on the capsule wall
like wings and breathe
while thousands of drops of water travel my body
make their way via gravity to the ocean.
In the centre of this vast, public building I am
an astronaut of privacy.

You used to yell in my face
instead of watching the road
while we veered and strained against our seatbelts
and in the back the dogs were thrown against the windows.
And you punched a hole in the bathroom wall
by my head, while I was covered in soap
or that's how I remember it
that I could feel the suds on me.

On anatomical charts you see the body as its parts
the tongue with its blue tentacles swimming
geology of skin in all its layers.
*The eye is just a ball of jelly* my doctor told me
as he looked right through it
to where – I guess I am not surprised –
he could see my brain, that meaty cloud.

# FEMALE FAMILY ANNIHILATORS

Standing on the field while other people's daughters
play sport, their limbs and tragic just-appearing breasts
little lumps of fat on their chests.

I see someone I don't really know, but remember
when she broke her arm; it seemed so out of place
to see a grown, raw-faced woman in a plaster cast.

From here you can see our house, you can barely see our house
it had to conform with the city's need for it to be invisible.
We clap and people call out: *Dribble!*

In sports fields built on rubbish dumps, items may surface
like a friend who'd pull slivers of glass from her mouth
relics of a car crash years before.

Female family annihilators are probably not that angry.
I feel they might just be trapped
inside the body of their lives.

I'm back at home now with the knives
my grandma got when she left the factory.
If you hold them to the light you see steel inside the bone.

I don't know.

# CATALOGUE

The sour smell of towels, flannels
left hanging over shower glass.
Mattresses in too-small rooms.
Chicken blood rotting in the rubbish drawer.

I gave a little girl my Daphne.
*I like things that smell nice*, she said.
And: *sometimes I smell my fingers.*
We left it there.

I remember now the smell of ashes
in the grate of my old fireplace.
And baby oil. Hot bathwater.
A band-aid with its red strand of cotton.

Mouldy citrus in our wash house
grapefruit shipped
from Grandpa's tree
in cardboard boxes.

And in order hard to call:
neck, head, morning,
still-day ocean, pillow,
cunt and cinnamon.

# HOW TO BE HAPPY THOUGH HUMAN

From the Circle there was a man we couldn't see
just his fingers held out for emphasis
like the hands of a preacher
or a primary school teacher.

Before that we had been at the film
where three people taxidermied a baby zebra
caught in the moment of standing
for the first time.

I go back to the wings
of the stage of my school's assembly hall.
Smell of dust and afternoons.
We are hiding from folk dancing, which we love.

And I go back to Saturday
we dance with other people
other people's children,
create *community* with physics.

Memory is a kind of mourning.
We take each other's hands
as if they were made for that
and we form a circle.

# WALKING UP THE ZIG ZAG

Walking up the zig zag
a harbour behind me
an ocean if you think of it
and mountains, going by the name of hills.

Someone has been along to paint
the railings, white on the cut-back ivy
you sometimes see a patch like that
on the wings of a tūī.

On the whole I disapprove
my neighbour's houses,
hard to reach, hard for the sun
to reach. A bulge of foam

where someone tried to seal
a leaking window.
A trailer with its freight
of dirt-filled plant pots.

Even their street numbers:
the three here is upside down
its tail at the top and stub
cutting short at the bottom.

A childhood friend lived there
in that sad apartment
facing south, her baby coughing,
she was not a good person, but still.

I turn for home. No wind.
The smell of grass, of night coming on.

There's no one, just my body,
that faithful one, for company

I take the last few turns in darkness
steep, short of breath
these legs have been mine all my life.
Hot hands. Small nights within my lungs.

We are fortunate to live in a world.
We are fortunate to live in a world
where some person, some man
is painting railings on the zig zag

and when he finished
he could have raised his eyes
and seen, beyond the black-tree hills
some ragged and fast-moving clouds.

# BAFFIN ISLAND

The origins of the decade, I was going to say,
were a small house with a very limited number
of powerpoints, enough energy for a bygone era
but not nearly enough for today so each outlet
was forced to grow a coral reef, a barnacle, a *burl*
of double plugs each piggybacked on the others
with a sense of day-to-day precariousness, domestic
danger being both the most lethal and least interesting;
but that was twenty years ago, I see with a start,
this decade had its genesis in an even smaller house,
like the world's tallest river barge, its prow a bay
of stained glass and daisies and the great thing,
my father said, about those windows is you can clean them
with a toothbrush; *that* was where the decade began
in the house where the neighbour, in despair,
would put her head through the sash window to complain . . .
but no, wait, it wasn't that house either, if I have recourse
to the facts (unusually) the house where I started the decade
was the house in the dead end street that once a year
looked out on pōhutukawa just blasting red like the roofs
of a bunch of needly circuses, and the man from the halfway house
at number eight who came and did an enormous shit
– in the toilet, but still – and the room we slept in, our room,
as I suppose any person would say, was not big enough
so we were breathing and rebreathing and then
the dehumidifier came and took the sweat and breath of our bodies
from the room in clear buckets smelling like nothing at all
one after another, *that* was the house of ten years ago
with its floors that came up beautifully and its porch
where I played for hours with my nephew and its garage door
that often had a wētā trapped in it, like some Greek
monster guarding the threshold to another world,
because that was my writing garage, and from there I could see

the spy base, and the gulls circling the rubbish dump,
and the infinitely complex leaf city of the tree,
those classical icons of my start-of-that-decade poetry:
so it was there that the decade opened, and love
took the form of a man who placed his duplicate cheese grater
in a box without a backward glance and settled in to watch
the top of the news and late in the night, under the wide rectangle
of the window above our bed, the outlet of next door's heat pump
would hum and whirr, hum and whirr, and we were utterly immune
sleeping together became something we were exceptionally good at
within the sealed cells of our insulating black-out blinds,
and it was in that room that I said one morning, I smell . . .
mouldy citrus fruit – as if that might be the symptom
of some kind of brain issue – and you went to the wardrobe
and took out your satchel and took out a plastic bag and took out
a mouldy mandarin and the look on your face was one of wonder
like I had pulled the sword from the stone: that was where the decade
began. We had a map of Baffin Island in the toilet – *National
Geographic* – and I never grew tired of looking at that icy
archipelago against its pale blue arctic sea.

# BEACH HOUSE

I discern the weather by watching the river
the small patch I see from the kitchen table.

If it resembles ranges of blue brown mountains
it's too windy to go to the beach.
If it's dully fawn and silver, it's a grey day
when the sand and sky will feel the same.
If the river is golden, maybe I haven't even seen it
maybe it's only been reported to me by my sister
who was getting in the washing during a spectacular sunset.
Maybe I'm in the bedroom with its hessian wall
not even seeing the rose gold sunset river.

This summer, one night, there was a house
parked up by the beach.
They were getting ready to move it somewhere
and it waited on the back of a truck
with a sign saying OVERSIZE and a wonderful view
down the creek to the sea, to Kāpiti, and beyond
where fishing boats haunt the night horizon like UFOs.

When you live long enough you know what houses are
how they become, in an instant, pathetic
a kind of unhaunting. Maybe someone has died,
there's been a crime, or maybe you're just moving,
you've packed up everything except a last telephone
trailing its cord to the wall.
You see things you never wanted to see
the lush, unworn edges of carpets
pale spaces behind pictures
or just the small human efforts that are made
the stacks of this and that
which in the end you know, can't hold anything back.

The opposite is your home in the dark
when you walk to the toilet in the moonlight
your furniture a Monument Valley
shadowed outcrop of the fridge
sofa afloat like a barge
your soft bare feet on the silvery floor
as if you crossed the frozen surface of a lake
or the surface of the moon itself
its cool, barren, transcendent powder.

*from* UNFAMILIAR LEGENDS OF THE STARS

## LARGE HEART FATAL

History shows
that people with an abnormally large heart
are prone to sudden cardiac arrests.

In the cool night
dogs bark in tune,
cicadas are dead quiet.

A free budgie
is lighthearted;
unlikely to survive the winter.

I think of drawing curtains
though it will take more than dawn
to wake me up.

# IN YOUR ABSENCE

In your absence
I stubbed out my arm.

Parcelled myself off
to various chaps.

I put the dog's head in a bucket
and she barked my shin.

I put my head down, received
brief papery epiphanies.

Enjoying a thermos of tea
in the Australian Garden

I thought – this is very fine, and –
no one is coming to rescue me.

# POSTCARD

Hope weather is good etc all is well and dog is wagging.

I thought, being beautiful, nothing could hurt you.

In Greece men hiss from doorways.
The mountains are high and particularly chilly.
Everything is slow slow.
The coffee is very bitter.

If you had married, goats might have nibbled your train,
a shepherd removed a hunk of cheese from his pocket.
The marble of your apartment would be valueless as plastic.
No one would understand but stare instead.

In the Hokianga with my mysteries –
*Goodbye Pussy, Swing Brother Swing* –
I am a small world away.
Still I say – all strength

And you were too good
And you were too good
And you were too good for him anyway.

## PICKY

You will despise me for rejecting
that glass. I will knowingly reject
it and select one not chipped not
sharpened in that way encouraging
slips of the tongue and lip. Perhaps for
your pleasure you would have me bite
the slick shattery side consuming it
like a circus act as entrée to
a steam train and side orders of thin
bicycles but madame will not be
performing tonight. There will be no
feats of endurance swimming no high
teetering or taunting of lions.
And when I am in the caravan
stitching sequins to strained outfits or
calming jet-lagged elephants out in
the straggly paddock the very least
I need is the clean rim the perfect
ring the edge of the glass smooth as skin.

# THROUGH HARDSHIP TO THE STARS

*for Mark*

It is a pleasure to order spices,
and good policy to empty out unknown powders.
I smile at a jar; once I was happy to write flour on its label.
Then, eyes moved in the head, skin wore off,
recipes were stained through overuse.

At the k-k-k-kitchen door
you tell me I'm your patron saint
and recite your Hamilton high-school motto:
Latin blah blah blah:
Through Hardship to the Stars.

In the pantry, sugar is crunching under cans,
a jar of gherkins requires urgent attention,
nutmeg is trailing from its packet.
So I send you off with a red apple
and return to my powders,
resisting the urge to alphabetise:
cardamom, cayenne, cinnamon, cloves.

# LEARNING EXCHANGE

Lessons are never
free but can be
exchanged.

I teach:
touch typing;
how to lose your friend;
the correct way to strike
a match.

I learn:
giving way;
basic clouds;
the electrical activity of
the heart.

I hope:
there is a Stephen Hawking of this
space, stuttering every dimension,
speaking out the stars and ways and emptinesses,
saying the vast dog's breakfasts,
the twins and swords and banished saints,
uttering trees that fall with no one to hear,
laying out a luminous point beyond the petty planets.

I fear:
I have nothing to teach, just utensils
laid out in a damaging row:
fish slice, corer, crusher, peeler,
an instrument for removing the heart of a pineapple,
bone handles and bamboo skewers, meat hammer,
Tupperware and pastry brush, still nothing has been preserved,
there is nothing laid down for the winter.

# WHEN ANIMALS ATTACK

As one unfortunate Texas family discovered
the polar bears can reach you as others watch in horror.

It never pays to be close to the gorilla.
Screws will weaken at the back of a mirror.

*Pre-plan emergency strategies!* I strangle out.
*Avoid. Reduce. Mitigate.*

In my sleep
the dead pay visits.

They have a warning tone, cannot stay long,
but hover by cigarette machines,

proffer recipes of unsure quantity,
hum *the sailor is home from sea.*

When animals attack
I am relying on logic: that chimpanzee

may spit your finger back
to be placed in chilled milk and reattached.

# LAZY EYE

On the way to Waikanae, Mum and Dad and Mary would say,
*look at the swans, Kate, look at the swans*, but I never saw one.
*Can't you see them?* they cried,
but weren't really surprised, as I'd always had a lazy eye.

Holidays passed and I pressed my face to the glass
looking in the flax for white feathers and curved necks.
There was nothing but a crowd of grey-green spears
and flax-heads heavy with seeds.

One day I was reading *Little House on the Prairie*
when a voice in the car said, *can't you see the swamps?*
And at that instant a thousand birds flew up
and circled wide as planes beyond my vision.

# EXCHANGE

Magnolia heads turn away,
a card reads –
*I've been working my arse off*
I stand, scanning the box for more.
There are nubs of blossom
and a fly enacting
a roundabout version of summer.

At the Post Office I use a pen
chained like a plug
to address my usual gurgle,
maybe suck you in.
I send it to a photograph of you
crowded by monuments
at the start of your winter.

# UNFAMILIAR LEGENDS OF THE STARS

The wind turbine propels a sky
fighter grey above.

*The tallest angel's head*
*curved the night.*

A liquorice cable
wires hand to mouth.

*Proud magpies*
*raced the dawn home.*

Asphalt remains lively
weeks after its laying.

*The water-girls laughed*
*and were exiled.*

Things happen
and are wrapped in newspaper.

*A seamstress sewed a spirit*
*from a girl's skin.*

I put a ring around your name
and circle the globe.

# TO TELL MYSELF SEVEN STORIES
# ABOUT ME AND YOU

1

He is in the desert, rolling up the sleeves of a rough-fabric shirt to spin
the propeller of a plane that is covered in dust. She is there, disguised as
a camel or nurse, creeping up to write 'clean me' on the powdered wing.
Somewhere, brass ornaments are being purchased, detailed trays for
bearing tiny glasses of coffee, and hash boxes with ill-fitting lids.

2

In the unremarkable town people gather at a Post Office. She is placing
letters on her tongue like stamps and feeling them dissolve. They leave a
taste in her mouth and when she sees him next she spits the letters back.
An 'e' and two capital 'R's stick at the corner of her lip. He laughs as he
picks up the stamps, the letters, the broken words gummed to the floor.
He moulds them into a tidy blob, the kind you find under school desks
and chairs. She forgets to notice what he does with it.

3

There is something she is very sorry about. Around and around she goes,
reading the names of roses. He is not a gardener and so has no reason
to be there, among the ovals of cut branches. But he likes to see the
mechanism. Pruning. *I've travelled the world and I've never tasted a better
prune* the man says on the advertisement, but deep inside she knows he is
lying. Amberlight. Katherine Mansfield. Benson & Hedges. Peace.

4

He follows her to the Chinese supermarket. As she chooses her
fireworks he sneaks behind her, slipping crackers into her coat pocket.
Friendship. Bridal Veil. Known Mountains of the World. She is too

clever for him though, too clever for them both. She leaves her jacket in the aisle, and carries the fireworks in the front of her jersey, which she holds out like a pelican. A shop assistant slips when a dozen Emerald Fires spill near the checkout.

5

When he goes on his trip, he doesn't take any bags. All his worldly belongings he ties about his body with string so he resembles nothing so much as an enormous puppet show. Some people think to throw him coins as he stops to catch his breath in the airport, but can't find a hand or a hat out anywhere. She sees him, of course, from behind a glass of Fanta, she can see him amongst all that stuff and he looks nice orange. She sucks up the picture of him with a straw.

6

In back country he is sitting on a half a petrol drum. She is pointing at a waratah singing *when the stakes are high it doesn't pay to sit on the fence* to the tune of the *Sesame Street* song, which she knows he particularly dislikes. Never mind, she is gone off now, and he is looking, looking, trying to make stuff out. He does a few neat tricks with his hands and a blade of grass. Later, when light has gone down, he can make out the stars clear as day but it's little consolation and no meat and veg.

7

Passing him on the street, she fails to recognise herself and someone else says hello to him instead. Cool Hand Luke went to jail for cutting the heads off parking meters, she remembers. Taking the shortest route between two points she feels like an idiot now, for all the foolish things she plans to do in the future. Thumbed books offer their approving faces and she rushes in to Poetry and inhales some little-read pages of Donne, which smell particularly good. Lovely stiff pages like starched dust.

*from* REALIA

# PERSONAL EFFECTS

I went to the Kilbirnie Watchtower to pick up your personal
effects from a policeman with your name.
The faint sun made me sweat a little in the car
in my cream rabbit-fur jacket you've never seen.
The policeman was absent so a woman not in uniform
gave me the brown envelope, the size of a foot,
and I held it against my stomach, in the fur,
as I walked back out to the car.

And there wasn't much in it:
a wallet, and $3.15 in change, and a white cigarette lighter.
It was all there, as they'd promised,
and the lighter was still going strong,
good as new, and the wallet from Kingston Leather was soft
and moulded like someone made a cast of your pocket,
and there were cards in there, a tiny stack of cards, so I laid
them out in a line on the table and didn't really try to divine
anything from them.

There was a student ID, community services card and a ten-trip
bus ticket, three sections, with one clip left on it.
There were copy cards, national and city library cards
and phone cards and one card read IRIDOLOGY:
EYES SHOW OUR ENTIRE BODY'S HEALTH.
And I looked to see which sector of the iris denoted irony
and which despair but the closest I could find was
Reality Coping and Chest Cavity,
and then, just as I was about to put the cards away,
I saw the little key that showed the location of the heart –
according to iridology – right in close to the pupil.

# UNFINISHED LOVE THEOREM

Like light
it can travel in waves
or lines
depending on the circumstances.

When I first noticed it, it was travelling in waves
and I could just see its sail pop hopefully up
on the horizon now and then
as it was keeling, or gibing,
or doing whatever brave ocean craft do
when the water is a little lumpy.

I admired its buoyancy, its neat fittings,
the way everything a person could need
was stowed in its purpose-built compartments.
I liked the way it was rigged, and aligned
with particular stars and magnetisms.

Now I'm in amongst it, I find it is travelling in lines,
the underground veins of a railway, hidden,
signposted, never drawn to scale on maps.
It is moving all sorts of things about,
taking good folk to their work, taking them out
and home to their rumpled bedrooms.

I admire its secret progress, how it can speed
or lull you on its beating window,
how it spills you out up silver
stairs and it's unexpected sun, or night lights
shining, seeming so bright, so very surprising.

# WATER OF THE SWEET LIFE

We can lie suckered against
each other so when I move
I peel my skin off you, hear
it pull away. I can hold
part of you in the dark and
not be sure what part it is:
we are a confusion of
limbs, like a pride of lions
only lazier and more
golden. I can hear and make
sounds with no words can
venture into your mouth can
do all this but when I climb
off the boat and on the sea
green lino go my daring
feet tippy toeing to the
toilet I piss with perfect
delicacy behind closed
doors decanting against the side
of the bowl as if I were
that unctuous Indian
waiter pouring your Kingfisher
never spilling a drop.

# REALIA

while you are talking
I am planning

what to say
when you stop

I turn words around
can't quite get it right

we are all speakers of other languages
dialects of accidental harshness

ways of failing
to be understood

and it's a well-known fact
that the grammar of sadness

is fiendishly difficult
full of rules, and exceptions to rules

full of except,
only when, and if

so forgive me, I can only say
*it is a beautiful castle*

*my leg is broken*
*and that is very expensive*

# THE SPINE GIVES UP ITS SADDEST STORIES

I pay a man to manipulate me.

He lays out a sheet of clean tissue
cradles my head and says
from behind a Swiss moustache,
*Have you had accidents before?*

*Oh yes, I want to say,*
*I am the very devil for injury*
*I disguise myself*
*as a white line and live on the road.*

I do not say this, I lie
prone in a curtain room
the William Tell overture
plays at quiet volume

his chest is warm on my back
my head is heavy in his hands
there are tiny clicks happening inside me
that even he doesn't know about:

the secret language of the spine.

# THE VILLAGE

I live in a block called The Village.
We are without a blacksmith, but not
without caring. Some evenings ago
a window shattered and seven doors
– of a possible sixty-nine –
opened to be seven times concerned
if helpless in our dressing gowns.

So when yesternight, as I listened
to positive thoughts on a tape and
willed my spine to align, I heard a
man shout, 'You're breaking my fucking heart,'
I knew I'd not be alone in caring.

From up here, he was a baseball cap
with feet. She was invisible, her
vocal cords tearing, her voice a child's
first attempts to play the recorder.
'Just fuck off,' she told him and as if
in some Elizabethan play he
mirrored her, 'No, you fuck off,' he said.

By this time, sillhouettes had gathered
on balconies across the way. Lights
were popping on like cardboard windows
on an advent calender. 'You don't
know what you're losing,' he yelled from beside
a roadside fig tree, 'you don't know what
you're fucking losing.' And then, silence.

A few minutes later, I heard his
footsteps, knew his gait by now as one might
know the shape of a man once loved

and never forgiven. Quietly, I heard
a soft knock, a key turn, a door
breathe open and gently close.

They are there together now, somewhere
muffled in the concrete stomach of
The Village, curled in their disastrous
nest, perhaps stabbing one another
to death, or having sex, or smoking
fat, greasy joints in front of the telly
exhausted and broken and hanging together.

I have a new summer blanket of
pale lime green. I relax the muscles
around my eyes and visualise
my vertebrae in perfect alignment.
I am all alone up here and safe
– oh safe – and I will never take their place.

# A PRIVATE GEOGRAPHY

One may never travel peacefully
to the hot countries lovers abandon
you for, to the ugly capitals
where they were born and whose name they claimed
over and over telling you all
about their distant self while you watched
their lips part like the petals of a
foolish flower spreading sounds just to
move their mouth around, close to yours.

Just as one always knows the letters
of one's first numberplate, I would not
drive a Holden or a Subaru,
they would remind me of you. I will
never own a car of navy blue,
will never buy again from a man
deep in the dusty heart of his yard
shadowed by a darkening shelter belt
hitching his trousers and saying from
behind his hand, 'She goes sweet, sweet as,
sweet as a rose.'

Quite ruined of course
are many stretches of road, sand dunes,
doorways and alleyways and ways of
doing things, certain jokes and puns have
palled, whole districts of the city, bays,
hillsides, innocent roadways alive
with letterboxes are lost to me.
I would as likely visit them as
name my child after him, or him.

If like school pupils stopped on the street
for research we were called upon to
draw a map of the world we would mark
in first the sectors most dear, islands
of no great signficance drawn
a hundred times their natural scale.
Knowing well the troubled countries of
the heartland we would score deep into
the paper their disputed borders.
Studies show that love, like geography
is a science that starts where we are.

# NEW YEAR

On the last night of the year it was extraordinarily warm.
We carried our jackets down the street like the pelts
of newly killed animals and kept mentioning,
in a wondering tone, the word Australia.

Through the lighted doorway of a house we saw
men on the floor praying to Mecca
which was in the direction of the Newtown shops.
They wore white caps like the caps of supermarket butchers.

We walked past beer bottles left on letterboxes.
In a street quite dauntingly empty a man said to you,
'Fuck I hate it when I see someone walking
with a beautiful woman.'

At the apartment you looked at pictures and I admired
the uncut cheese, huge and grey and solemn.
Little fireworks were going off like warning shots.
Suddenly the year was nearly gone and we were hurrying.

At the moment it tipped over we were standing
holding hands by a concrete block as large as a car.
We looked at one another and smiled and kissed:
you kept your tongue in reserve. I said nothing.

When the rain started to fall it was with a certain grace.
You had always been one favoured by the elements.
Arriving home sober and just a little damp it was an empty
year with no days in it. Just one warm evening too still to last.

# MIRAGE

It was the kind of day on which you might expect to find
a soft, dead bird exquisitely brown and curled at rest like a leaf.

At the zoo the giraffe stood in its doorway,
its legs bent like a harp, its movements kindly.

Two zebra nibbled in the mud.
A more brown than yellow lion looked out at the rain

falling straight down from the sky.
The lion looked left and it looked right.

Across at Miramar the three white petrol tanks
were reflected like a temple, like the Taj Mahal.

Their shape was of the most simple
and substantial kind.

Down and down we walked, I and I
each alone we walked into the darkest woods.

I knew not the names of birds going off like sirens.
Trees like the backbones of fish.

There was mist.
Nothing would be landing.

Down on the street
someone was selling a mirage.

## ADMIT ONE

Cranes like cranes above the city.
The city is a poem that says

no matter what boat you take
you cannot find

the boat to take you from yourself
to yourself.

The man who is part
of a boat

disguised as a sailor
in blue and white

writes the name of the poet
on a ticket

admit one
it says.

A long way from Constantinople
a long way from love the poem

is chilled in the air
conditioned bookshop

it is about lips and kings
and ruination.

The frivolous can call me frivolous
the poem says

I have always taken important things
extremely seriously.

# STARS WITHOUT MAKEUP

Something smells like burning
in the back room
you say.

I just don't think I should have to
I checked every letter
I'm not attached to anything.

\*


When I came home you left me petrol
straight black hairs on the floor

and a poem on the back of something
more important

a plan to meet
a note a place a person.

There was an envelope of money
on the table that shone like a still, brown lake

all those pictures of the Queen and only one
of you and me.

\*


At night I look up
the sky is full of stars
without makeup.

\*

And where was I going with this story?
something about the girls I knew

at the tops of mountains
they could only feel the air
and how little air was in it

they were all so beautiful and
exhausted.

*from* BEAUTY SLEEP

# LUCKY

You can always tell the lucky people
they are the ones who say
you make your own luck.

Certain songs have the sound of ringing phones
and some make you think
there is a knock at the door.

When you move the clock
you always look for the time
at that same empty place

and so it is
something removed
not calling or knocking

and when people climb onto the bus
they say
*Do you go past the hospital?*

Then you find you don't care about the hospital
anymore. There is that pink
concrete house, the wedding cake

and cars glitter on distant roads
like the shining tops of waves
and spray their water spouts like whales

and in your mouth, in that small night,
there are teeth lined up like rows
of sleeping houses

you have built hotels
on all the most important properties
and kept them close to your tongue.

# GUESTS

You left behind a crown
of flowers, a hairclip with teeth like claws
and a red wine stain resembling the Qantas sign.

When it seemed to me the sky was getting violet
I tried to hide the clock. No matter, its face was dark
and its menacing tick hidden by music.

And so, yo ho, we were not as drunk as sailors
but kept our watch from the sofa
which swam through the night like a boat.

And when you left you were two dark heads below
the balcony, you were two underneath the white sign of a taxi
and I was one, delighted, with dozens of glasses in front of me.

# ANYONE CAN BE A MAGICIAN

The golden age of the freak
did not begin until the 1840s.

Married couples of oddities.
A moving theatre of the extraordinary human body.

The woman in the row in front
claps with sad, urgent stiffness

red knuckles
hands like birds fighting.

Her friend over-laughs
leaning forward as if vomiting.

I give a start when a girl behind
drops her ring on the wooden floor.

We came and saw a clown here once.
He affected sadness – even died – on the stage

but when we saw him later at the bar
every line of his face was warm as a baby.

We leave and the night smells of pencils
all that blackness, scribbling.

The farthest things
in the universe are hugely energetic

and we are the cries of headphones
when they fall out of your ear

and yes, when you were growing up darling
none of this was here.

# HAMILTON INTERNATIONAL AIRPORT

*New Zealand is the Saudi Arabia of milk,*
said the taxi driver.
*When I came back I just about kissed*
*the green grass.*

He had driven trucks in America,
*the whole place has got wheels*
*it takes twelve hours to drive across Texas.*

In the back seat I was experiencing a top ten hangover,
had stumbled in the air bridge when boarding.
*Oh, America,* I said.

The Waikato was going past
its roadside grass
its bridges and signs and fences.

*The thing is,* he confided, *experience.*
*Experience will always beat the young fullas.*
*In America New Zealand is like Fiji is to us.*

The little house grew near. We passed the massive tree
with its dappled bark, we passed the KFC.

At the end of my street you could almost cry to see the trees
that reached across and touched in the middle
and the tiny lawn the size of a pair of sheets.

*Here you go,* he said, *we happen to be a nation*
*that has carried out a lot of its history in sheds.*

# A TRIP TO AUCKLAND

The air was warm and dark, warmer and darker.
By the carousel we waited
we were touching and it seemed I leaned
on you though perhaps you leaned too
against me; anyway it was good.

Men in shining jackets stood on the motorway
by orange lights. They barred our way
then showed the bright green sign that said GO.
GO, I thought, GO.
It was like a foreign language.
Everything was new to me
I knew nothing of roads and streets.

The house was light and moved when we did.
With my arm above my head as I lay
I might have been a ballerina
bent over in a music box.

Outside insects or maybe frogs
were making the noise of phone calls.
Vertical blinds drifted like bars
being moved for a great escape.
When you slapped a mosquito against the wall
you shook the place.

Before dawn the neighbour left in his truck.
You said he was heading to Cape Reinga
and I tried to imagine what he would take there
in a truck, what he would deliver.

When morning came it was clean
and seemed to arrive not from the normal

place that days come from, it was extraordinary
and so we went into it, stepped out to join
that ocean of traffic.

We never got to go ice skating
though there was a rink
you had told me about
where I would need to wear
long trousers and not fall over.
I imagined us as in a film, flying down some frozen river.

When I boarded the flight I was starving.
Like a prisoner I waited for food
and when it came the knife and fork and spoon
were freezing.

# RUSSIAN CARAVAN TEA

*Don't know why but I'm feeling so sad,*
said the walkman.

We had dangled its tiny earpiece
over the mouth of a plastic champagne flute

this was our stereo
the stillness of the wooden caravan.

*I long to try something I've never had,*
Billie Holiday was singing

and we could hear her well enough
under the silent stars.

Once you had died and we had done those things –
visited the apricot room

and smoked our mouths to hot
caves – I went under the knife.

The anaesthetic took me down
and surgeons pulled the very eyes from my head.

When I came to, the world was in the wrong place
and the wrong place was me.

In a photograph you are eating muesli
with your feet in the water of the Hokianga.

I stood behind with the camera
called your name, *Mark*

*look back*, I said,
*look back over your shoulder.*

# THE INSOMNIAC LEARNS A LOT

Dark voices talk to her
about the most poisonous substance
known to man, about heirloom potatoes
and for an hour acute pain.
Next week: chronic pain.

All around her tiny green, red and orange lights
where things are in sleep mode and standby mode.
The house is a city full of traffic
needing to be told when to stop and go.

Underneath the covers her body is busy
and warm as an animal.
So many litres of sweat drain out of it
she might drown in her mattress
might lie in it like a tank
like a glass coffin.

All night the house ticks and clanks
like a cake cooling on a rack.
With its curtains drawn it is blind
and only two eyes open
only two doll's eyes fighting open.

In the morning men come to break bottles
men come to cut, they leap from their truck
and mow down hundreds of daisies
that at night close up like fields of fists
because even flowers
know how to go to sleep.

## YURI GAGARIN'S BED

Have you ever had the urge
when zipping up a high-necked jacket
to simply keep on zipping
to capture the fine membrane of the throat
in those plastic dovetailed teeth
eliminate the face and package yourself
in an instant for disposal?
I never have. Just a simple question.

After the storm we went walking.
The river had moved – nothing unusual in that
and the driftwood piled knee deep
was like treading on a giant nest.
After a storm in the 1970s here
my grandmother nearly fell into the creek.
What a thrill that was.

What was new to even the most jaded aesthetic
were the hundreds of onions washed up on shore.
Roused from fields by the flood
they were in unsanitary condition
and not suitable for cooking
the council had advised.
They were excellent for kicking.

Did you know that Yuri Gagarin
spent the night before his space flight
in a single bed in the Baikonur Cosmodrome?
Its head had four steel bars as if he slept in a small prison
and it was covered in a thin blue and white coverlet
with a pattern like a china plate.
There was one white pillow at the end
geometric as a pellet of chewing gum.

Yes folks I'm afraid this world has a habit
of disappointing. When you go to watch the fireworks
they are never as big as the ones overseas
even when you are overseas.
Personally I like the ones that are slow and golden
like drifting smoothed-foil Easter egg wrappers
and last for so long, whole lovely seconds.
I watched a display one time
with a man who no longer loved me
and when they finished, he took my hand
and we walked home in the rain.

I don't know.

## SIX WEEKS

Six weeks was all that remained of my life.
In apartment number three I farewelled
the young Prince William who had visited
bringing a plastic bag of half-finished cigarettes.
I considered restarting the habit in my last days
but decided against it, based on the smell.

Walking along the beach with everyone
I ever knew, I noted a number
of sweet, humble cottages, went on ahead
(past even my mother, who led the procession)
to be alone and sob for the fact. I felt sorry
for my friend: to lose first her son and then me.

*What was it?* you asked in the morning,
*what were you dying of?* and I felt the word swoop
into my mouth the way a bird flies across the sun.
*Oh, it was cancer,* I said,
and folded my arms over my chest
like the heavy wings of an angel.

# LAWNS

On the mower's handle the white shapes of two animals
the tortoise and the hare
that one might know how fast to travel
using fables as a guide.

To start the mower with the pull cord
is like performing some harsh butchery of nature
the cruel energy of a birth
or a clean break of a crooked limb.

In Harry's garden, he explained the Wandering Jew
was less offensively known as Wandering Willie.
His guide to the regional names of New Zealand weeds
remains, I believe, unpublished.

Sometimes I would try and try the mower
my arm becoming weak
and Harry would come down from the house
in his thick glasses and pull the cord for me.

The perfect contrast of strength and weakness:
he with as little air as might stay in a balloon
days after the party
could still pull more powerfully than me

that single explosion
the arm
part of the engine
to sputter and cough the Flymo to life.

Beside him I was grandiose, my legs in boots
a force of nature. I would listen,

learned to look into the distance
while he wheezed and caught his breath.

He would tell how he had rowed
across the Sound, had shovelled gravel
and once seen Vincent vomit in his coat sleeves
when holding the iron railings of the gardens.

Up and down I walk this careful Rover
its catcher like a humpback whale.
It leaves the lawn looking like a sack
a little brown and barren.

Not like the Flymo
which really did fly across the bank
you would feel like an artist or warrior
with that at the end of your leash

its powerful mouth and skilful obedience
and when one day a man up a power pole said
*You're doing a good job there*
I knew I was.

# BEAUTY SLEEP

Tiny fangs of yachts
in the channel.

Last night I felt an earthquake
it shook the house
like someone sitting down
suddenly on the edge of the bed.

Walking up the path one time
I thought you'd hung a blue sheet on the line

it was the sky

that today wears the white and ragged half circle
of the moon
like the trace of a peeled-off price sticker.

No word from the piano.
It is saying nothing
since I closed its dark brown mouth
the day you left for England.

*from* THE MIRROR
OF SIMPLE ANNIHILATED SOULS

# THE MIRROR OF SIMPLE ANNIHILATED SOULS

*Of the life which is called the annihilated life*

The annihilated barely make an imprint in this world
their beds are given away to others
they sleep suspended from the floor
by their own disbelief.


*How this Soul takes no account of anything that might be*

With great effort it resists the urge to count
the birds and flies that make fleeting
black lines across the world.
It neither springs forward nor falls back.


*How such creatures no longer know how to speak of God*

There was a time when he filled their mouths
with a mushroomy taste of semen
but that is not the same as understanding.


*How this Soul is compared to an eagle, and how she takes leave of Nature*

Like the great bird she is threatened by banalities
the growth of the suburbs and the ever increasing need for corn.
Ah! She takes leave of Nature by the most direct means possible
the world rising up to meet her, punctual death.

*How this Soul is balanced between two equal weights, and how she is drunk*
    *from what she never drinks*

What else is there to say? This world is heavy, she is its balance.


*How this Soul swims in a sea of joy*

Generations of waves approach laughing from behind
the world's tear enters and leaks from her.


*How the Soul has arrived at understanding of her nothingness*

Or she says she has.


*By what means the Soul has conquered, and how she is without herself*

She has conquered by these means: anger, teeth and looking.
She is without herself
as at the moment the door slams
with its key inside
with its lock upon the soft nerves of the fingertip.


*How it is necessary to die three deaths before one arrives at the free,*
    *annihilated life*

The first death is the sweetest, in its novelty round in the mouth.
The next is unremarkable, an act of forgetting.
The third death does not bear thinking about
the body is a cave
and the mind that primitive creature caveman.
No wonder we live in houses, wear clothes and run to the telephone.

*How the Soul sings and chants*

At all times music is entering and emerging from her.
She is a marvel of repetition, echoing joy
as the canyons of the desert echo.


*How this Soul is free, more free and very free*

Free by means of her own hand.
More free by the world, its affairs and schedules.
Very free by loneliness, that key
she jingles in her pocket like money.


*How the land of the sad is far from the land of the annihilated*

Do you want me to draw you a map?
It would be all borders
no countries.


*How the Soul is delighted by the suffering of her neighbours*

They live in the dark. They speak not in words but in sounds.


*How the Soul who has caused this book to be written*
*excuses herself for making this book so long in words,*
*which seems so small and brief to the Souls who remain*
*in nothingness and who are fallen from love into such being*

Apologies and excuses of course she doesn't mean them.
They pour from her like golden wheat.

# MUTE SONG

*i*

The first time I saw you
I don't know which I loved more
you with your tranquil neck
calmly transporting yourself through the world
or the one who followed you everywhere
trolling the dark waters like a hook.


*ii*

The strange thing was that
as each other's opposite and negative
we were even visible
I with my tatty winter coat
smelling of reeds
you consisting entirely of surfaces
or should I say one fabulously curved surface
smooth and white as an egg.


*iii*

I have no idea what you saw when you looked at me
a shadow dully pursued by the shape that cast it
a placeholder reserving a space from nonexistence.

Perhaps you saw God's fearsome ability
to be absent, his morosely taken option
to hoard his riches in another universe.

In anyone else, such a thought would be absurd.
In your case, it was luminous and adorable
shining in the dark location known as me.


*iv*


It was inevitable I would follow you
the sound of laughing that came
though you never laughed
the sweet nonsensical conversations
in which you remained impassively silent
the pointless journeys you took
your eyes perfectly round.

My desire was the desire to be superlative
I, who had spent years in domestic craft
became selfishly single-minded as an artist
inflicting your beauty on myself
like some ecstatic adolescent
cutting her arm with a pocket knife.


*v*


At night I would disappear.
You and the moon would glow.
I hated to think of the dark
covering you over like a mouth.

# DEEP NAVIGATION

The piano was something she played with her hands
her hands, of all things
it was full of tiny hammers dark
body of a whale
a piece of musical furniture
and she the Russian doll on a too-small

chair dedicated the song to her mother, small
turn of the head, her hands
not pressing the ivory furniture
but seeming to land and alight, things
at once heavy and weightless as a whale
moving through the ocean dark.

We listened in the dark
confines of the bar, that small
place below the surface, as in the whale
Jonah reached, his blind hands
touching not mere things
but the body's living furniture

that furniture
in which life sits at home in the dark.
It was one of those things
that when I searched the small
household of my bag I couldn't put my hands
on a pen so *piano whale*

was all I kept that night, *piano whale*
and how the furniture
was cut short so people rested their hands
on the floor, squatted in the dark,

a crowd of warmly dressed folk singers at small
stature. These are the things

I am saving, the things
that surface to breathe air like the whale.
In Alaska my father saw a small
grizzly emerge from the furniture
of its winter, its long dark
claws, its paws, its hands.

What are hands, are things
to that wintering bear, dark piano, whale.
The world, a doll's house with its small furniture.

# THE TIRED ATHEIST

In my hand I hold a mouse
a golden Labrador
and a cat, all the same size.

Yes I assume the mythical plenty of a god
where my eyes look become green hills
red houses, skies necessarily blue.

In Córdoba the smell of shit and orange blossom
TVs await the Pope, that puff of smoke
who knows what they burn to make it black or white.

Of course I don't want to live apart from God's grace.
What kind of idiot would force air from their lungs
or retch up water?

No, behold the mismade agonies
of those who attempt to hear with the tongue
or eat with the eyes, forcing crusts of bread under the lids.

Behold the quiet substance of their rooms
the hollow air in the cavities of their bodies
the finity of their lives, tasting like morning

now you tell me, if one knows everything
and one knows nothing
what the fuck are they going to talk about?

# GAMBLING LAMBS

I hardly know what to say to you
that I remained in clockless darkness
while outside you repeated yourself in broadcast loops
your sunlight falling on the overweight masses
with a democratic evenness that sucked the perspective.

That when I sought you in Paris, in Venice, downtown
you were not only absent but had erased yourself
leaving smudges on the faux marble columns
as if this world were your mere skirting board
your bumper car arena to be heedlessly marked.

I sought you in the desert, where water jetted high into the air.
I sought you in the desert, where monuments collapsed
beds and minute cum traces, sticky traces of liquor
reduced to constituent molecules.
God I felt lonely when I realised you were everywhere.

Pascal invented roulette to aid his research
how maddeningly joyless your knowing has made you
I would rather kill myself than hear another of your tricks
is this your card is this your card is this your card
as you split the thighs of the deck.

## DRIVING THE BYPASS

It was agreed the best thing for everyone
was that they cut my sister open.

I left the house after midnight
the warmest night of summer
the empty streets bursting
with green lights.

Outside Molly Malone's
a girl was walking home
carrying her shoes.

When I drove home it was dawn.
On the new bypass
I was suddenly thrilled
by all they had destroyed to build it.

The past, relocated, waited for me at traffic lights
and I drove at speed with everything
to be grateful for, the present minute
exploding and smashing
the past to dust.

I dreamed a red steam train
ran by my house
its cargo carriage upon carriage
of honeysuckle.

# DON'T GET ME STARTED

Wherever I went, there were maniacal screams
friends springing from behind couches.
Their hopeful faces arrived suddenly
then slowly fell, like fireworks.

Every minute was divided into chapters.
Having only moments
I never thought about the future
just – whoops – the constantly accidental present.

I appreciate the pleasure I gave others
my suffering a form of effervescence.
*The Human Bubbles!* I would bill myself
*The Man Who Can't Help But Make Music!*

In the solitary marathon of the night
I thought of when it all began:
morning air, concrete floor of the barn
the knife and neatly channeled blood

steaming as it gathered in a bucket.
Then, the first altercation with myself
like the first time a superhero
meets the one who becomes his nemesis.

Because people were full of helpful ideas
I began to hate them. *I have eaten a fucking pickle!*
I wanted to shout. *Don't talk to me about
digital rectal massage.*

The most astonishing thing was her love.
Like the sprigged blue and yellow flowers

of her nightgown
it was a constantly repeating small beauty.

The ordinary can be miraculous
if it happens often enough. Each moment
a calm object she placed in my hand
like a freshly unwrapped cake of soap.

*from* SNOW WHITE'S COFFIN

# THE LONELIEST OL' SONG IN THE WORLD

*i*

If this song ever saw the light of day it would fade real quick.

This is the song of axes falling.
And I say this is the song of axes falling
axes falling across a river.

This is the song of an eyelid
of an eyelid and of lemonade
and oh my love, how I fell into that lemonade.

The song inside a snowglobe thinks
*but it don't snow in Hawai'i*
and then it starts and turns the surfboards all to cake.

*ii*

One night, broke in Nashville, Willie Nelson was scratching around his
guitar looking to make the rent. Outside the window, lights were red,
green and red again. And green. And he was thinking about his sister,
his dead mom and dad and his grandparents' screen porch door, its
segmented negative Milky Way studded with flattened insects. He was
thinking about the future, how it would be different, would smell of
different sauces, *so many freaking sauces*, he was thinking. And it was
then that he stumbled upon this song, the loneliest ol' song in the world.
And I'd like to sing that to you now.

*Sweetheart when the axe is falling on that river*
*I am the sound that travels slow across the water*
*I am the runaway hiding in the forest*
*The petite forest called your hair and heart.*

*Sweetheart when time is falling in your eyes*
*That broken limb of time and tired bear*
*I am the one that wanders in the forest*
*And finds you in that forest, in the haunted forest of your hair.*

*Sweetheart when the snow is falling in your hand*
*I am the quiet bits of air it's falling through*
*And I am the quiet ground it's falling to*
*And I am the falling one and you are falling too.*

# ON READING GRAY'S *ELEGY WRITTEN IN A COUNTRY CHURCHYARD*

The morning air smells of leaves.
I see the paper in its plastic bag
the path overlaid with fine green moss
houses' windows white with curtains.

Beyond the neighbours' yard the hills
the white sphere of the spy station
and above, the white circle of the moon
about the same size.

\*


I saw my father on film the other day.
He was whatever age I am now.
He raised his eyebrows, clasped his hands
behind his back. He bent his body from the waist

as a crane might, or one of those novelty birds
that sips like a metronome from the side of a glass.
He smiled and moved his eyes around,
showing this side of the whites, and the other side.

\*


In the morning, on lovely mornings
when I step into that air
I expect to see a corpse
to be the one who discovers the body.

I can see it, face down on the neighbours' lawn
one arm above its head

its knee bent
as if climbing a wall of grass.

I look up to the hills
over where the dead body is not
to the spy base, the spider's egg
with the moon above it.

I don't want to leave this world.

# THERE IS NO EASY WAY

This is the way you will travel through the world
on feet, on arrangements of bones and body parts.

You will be standing on top of your shoes.
You will be walking inside the lining of your coat
and your fingers will poke through the frayed pocket lining.

Around the islands of your back teeth, rich with metals,
will be the liquids that you drink, disappearing down your throat.

There will be air inside you, an egg of it
inside your mouth, and a clam of it.

When you lie in the dark you will be nothing but a clock
spending your limited supply of minutes on minutes.
You will always be inside things, be they rooms, buildings,
or atmospheres, because there is no *outside*.

And I will tell you something, you will have animals inside you.
Two dark, dark bears, sleeping in a reek of their own urine.
Swans caught with their wings open like fountains.
And there will be raccoons, black eyes full of night time.
They feed on rubbish when they can't find a home in the woods.

## TO MYSELF

Precisely in the manner of Marcus Aurelius
I remain below the covers. You don't know this
how they smell of washing liquid

hold warmth in themselves as a body
that when I return from the kitchen
I open them as a body

they are not eating me they are not having sex
with me they are not giving birth to me
but they are a body for me and I for them

an item from that body
perhaps a thumb held within its hand
or two feet that keep each other company in the night.

Here within our clothes within our bedclothes
in our eyes our hairs and skins within this air
this particular envelope of air which might be made of space

except that it is made of time.
There are cooler patches of sheet to which I can apply
the inside of my knee.

I will put my hand beneath my ear
my eye will adhere to that place on the eyelid
that ancient injury, that when I wake

the fear of pain will make me hold the eyeball still
and not pursue a thought, a leaping deer.
The body is a coward, that is its job

to suck from the world its sugars
crawl into the slain bodies of monsters,
if necessary, to find a place to sleep.

# ONE HUNDRED AND FIFTY-ONE THOUSAND BRIDGES

It seems unlikely that, in its progress past the yet unbuilt floor
of an apartment building, a bucket containing a broom and a spade
can block out the sun. I am always surprised

to see leaves fall from the sky, mistake them for birds,
or plastic bags. Do you sometimes feel you might be painted
onto the world, find yourself standing

like an angel in a Dutch interior, with nothing to do?
You hold your hands in poses
as if playing invisible instruments

can't help but see the sleeping signs
of still life: a pomegranate lying on its side
a knife, a board, a loaf of bread. Do you see the world

there, its green hills and brown villages hanging on the wall?
Who knows what is really inside what, the room a doll's house
or the world a box, open up the cardboard doors

at last the day has come to see into the tiny countryside!
Watch me move across this chessboard with my angel feet
from behind you see the soles

turned backward like two lumbering beasts
far across a prairie.
History is taking place inside me, all its waste

young men exploding into trees
mining for silver and building bridges,
one hundred and fifty-one thousand bridges

# LETTER TO A FRIEND

The milk has frozen solid
its carton swelled like a pillow
and what you can pour from it, as it melts
is a thin white water.

I thought about you yesterday.
The park was full of children
barely visible in the dark
on thin poles they carried their lanterns
each with no flame inside
but small torches
bought by their parents for the purpose
or lightsticks, like pencils of colour.

One girl had lost her mother,
*I left her by the tree* she said,
as we looked into the invisible park
the greatest in this side of the city
built over a mountain of bunkers
that were smashed and filled with rubble
once the war was over.

We stood stamping while policemen stopped the traffic.
The carol-singing never started
but we walked back through the park
just the three of us
and Karla and Magdelena sang
and fully-clothed joggers
loomed out of, and back into, the mist.

After pizza we had bubble tea
the bubbles come up thick straws
like roe, you pop the sweet strawberry caviar

between your tongue and the roof of your mouth
the roof, as if the body were a building.
We all had the same feeling,
as if we were drinking the future.

It wasn't the future of course. It was the past. This is all the past.
That is why I can tell you about it:
because I crushed it in my mouth and destroyed it.

And thus concludes my letter. May I only add
that at the time I thought of you
the ground was thick with leaves
not yellow ones anymore, just soft and brown
like the patchy coat of an animal.

# SNOW WHITE'S COFFIN

Tom Waits records the sound of frying chicken
that's how he achieves his pops and crackles.
Our old unit had a hooked grey arm,
it was a trunk of wood with woven speakers.

As a child I worried about forgetting:
the hexagonal handle, a creamy honey cell,
that flaw in the lino resembling Donald Duck
while the others of its kind looked like grey bells.

Sometimes life would seem too big, even then
an empty Sunday where you drifted as a ghost.
I saw *Bonnie and Clyde* on such a day,
as I recall, in black and white

when the bullets came
they died like oceans
full of slow turbulence
as if brought by death to life.

Why preserve one's childhood memories?
So, like Egyptians, they might be packed into the grave?
That I would sit up nights, eating from the Haworth mug
spoonfuls of plain sugar mixed with cinnamon.

Is there room in the sarcophagus for that,
for the feeling of the covers of paperbacks,
in which girls survive, among great trees,
girls who make mistakes in forests.

One thing I loved was to pick the scabs on my knees
while sitting on the toilet.

Do I need to say, I ate them?
Who is taking this down?

\*


The Dutch I believe, have built a car one molecule long.
I've seen its silly form, its atom wheels.
It looks nothing like a car, it looks to be a pupa
some kind of baby bee surprised by disaster in its cell.

The problems of this world will not be solved by tiny cars.
Everything is small enough already
and there is too much, too much of everyone.
To understand your life you need another whole life.

I think we are sitting here on the axis my friend
that is why we feel a bit unwell.
Buried in us are minutes, days, mornings slept late
nights of no rest, turning to one side

turning again like a tide
sweating into the bodies of hot beds
those bucketfuls of moisture.
I think that futures might be in us too

driving in tiny cars, they are opening their minute glove
boxes and with infinitesimal hands
draw out maps too small to imagine
but they imagine them, they look at the lists of streets

all arranged according to the alphabet.
And then I think they throw the book away.
And they get out from the car
and they throw the keys into the ocean

howling. They do not want to go to places in books.
They will not drive
in their molecule cars
those ridiculous cartoons.

\*

Snow White's Coffin
is an integrated radio and record player
that introduced Plexiglas to the domestic interior.
Relieve yourself of the excruciating clutter of the world

is what it says to you
everything you thought was *being alive*
is revealed as a problem
which can be solved by good design.

## DOUBLE GLAZING

Once it is dark, there is no exterior.
Night becomes a means of reflection
you see room upon golden room
all in slightly wrong formation.

Something about light, about its properties
and the eye, which almost knows this, almost can
discern how this wall could be behind itself
a shadow and companion, that doors

which once by day appeared to open outward
start to open inward and within themselves
within again. You have seen a flower bloom in time lapse:
that is how doors are behaving in the window.

If people are to enter such a room, actual people,
they of course become their second selves. They loom
not out of darkness, but from a light so come-from-nowhere
it appears to be a darkness.

As they approach from the right they are seen from the left
and from the left the right, the *right*
as if one direction would always be
the home of knowledge.

When you maintain your watch
through night's medium
sized hours, blue morning comes.
This is what light will do:

Slowly take away the room
destroy its layers, its unexpected angles

its demonstrations of the laws of light and how light falls
and how the eye performs its tasks of understanding.

And so, when day is fully here, the window will be empty
that dolls' house theatre, that gold confusion
gone. There will only be the so-called outside world
going about its business made of sound.

# HISTORY AS SEEN THROUGH THE EYES OF BABIES

The dataset of the future:
What babies saw, in their orbits.

How their thoughts were outside windows
their thoughts were clouds passing by windows.

Their literature, barking of dogs in courtyards
faint songs transmitted through floorboards.

The history of babies is the history of people, rising and circling
as planets do.

As with the history of grown men
this history, history

as seen through the eyes of babies
is not without its grand conundrums

why death arrived too late
so long after everyone was born

and why the oceans, soft and woollen,
had never been harvested for their fur.

# SPREEPARK

*for Gaby Lingke*

We stood in a small field
among winter-dead yellow grass
the sun was shining on us from above
and we were casting no shadow
at least, the shadow we cast was beneath us
a pool, a root, a base, on which we were safe.

Taking up a lot of sky was the ferris wheel.
I didn't know then, but it would start to turn
in the wind, and make a sound
like the distant call from a muezzin.
As it turned through its circle
its red metal structures made a constant lesson
in geometry as the area of sky
within each shape gave itself over to the next.

A man walked his son towards the toilet
then stopped by the bushes
and pulled down the little boy's warm pants
so he could piss in the open air.
Later the same boy, with his small spade,
walked past staring up at me
he wondered why I stood, perhaps,
in the small grass field, looking at nothing,
what to him was nothing, the slow-moving wheel
and its companion, the chimney
creating and creating a roiling white cloud
like a time lapse of the weather
a pure, mesmerised pollution
utterly at home in an empty blue sky.

All the broken-down rides, the Grand Canyon
boats filled with leaves, the fallen dinosaurs
cars with ears, and the mouth of a cat
into which the rollercoaster disappeared:
you know about those. What you don't know
is that, in the small field, there are hedges
only knee high, and beyond them, behind a fence
the white shape that appears to be a mammoth
a broken mammoth, or a work in progress.
Trees leaning up against the sky like twiggy brooms.

It is true, many disasters may befall the human eye.
How can it be that we must walk through a world
with this little gelid world to lead us?
I thought you brought a telescope today
but it's your great-aunt's tripod, in its leather tube.
We are none of us sailors but I look to the horizon
above the kiosk and the heads of dog owners
waiting for the tour to begin, beyond the river
where the great chimney, alone,
is speaking its clouds into the sky.
We understand, you and I, that sunshine
is a form of time
and we stand in the small field
and watch it pass by.

# THE NIGHT SKY ON ANY DAY IN HISTORY

I want you to look into an oncoming night.
Is it a little green? Does it have the cool orange
beginnings of streetlights? Tip your head back
as someone with a nosebleed might.
Survey the lower sky. Are there chimneys
making mini city silhouettes? Satellite dishes,
their smooth, grey craters turned in one direction?

You might insist you hear a nightingale.
Might see, at a distance, the huge screen
advertising an upcoming concert by the Beach Boys.
You could spend your time watching trains pull
their strings of yellow windows along in lines.

Or you might come here, where I am
where I stand upon the rarely silent floor
looking up at the rectangle moon
of our neighbour's window.

# INTERRUPTED WORLD

You, neighbour,
waving your yellow towel

turning it into a yellow shirt
that you dress yourself in.

You fold your arms
or swing them like a signalman.

Can you imagine how your face might feel
to the air? How the hot summer wind

might shape itself around your blue-bruised calf
or the violet landscape of your hand veins?

The trees are giving off asterisks
pollinating you by accident.

And when the black military vehicle of a beetle
finds its way onto your skirt.

And when boats, travelling under bridges
are pushing heavy, empty barges.

And when dogs tremble
as they hover over their business in parks.

# UNTITLED POEM ABOUT MY NEIGHBOURS

My neighbours,
dear neighbours
your *interiors*
hung on the dark like paintings

each window a crucifix
here with a candle burning, here
the solitary lightning
of the television.

I don't want to know you but I want to know you
are there, trying on your red top
before the mirror.

And I want to hear you make mistakes
when you gather your friends round the piano.

I came up in a cage lift once, not here,
somewhere less efficient,
and I waited dumbstruck on the landing
by piano music from above
while in my hand the cold
carton of milk wept real tears.

I admit I watch you naked
your pale breasts
evoking all the *Playboy*s of my youth.

I never saw *Inception*
but I saw the city – it was Paris – turn in upon itself.
We've done that too

and though it took me years to see it
there's a kind of Sphinx
at the foot of the stairs
a dark green woman
with wings and claws

and there's the smell of the cellar
that basement smell
we are living on earth, then, after all.

*from* THE INTERNET OF THINGS

# THE INTERNET OF THINGS

I love the aesthetic of working ports
rust and containers
the way unwieldy ships move across the water
like buildings trained in deportment.

We need to accept that the world
is more intelligent than we are.
Like leaves on a tree we are something amazing
that behaves in predictable ways.

When we visited the childhood homes of the Beatles
they were, not surprisingly, heartbreaking.
I felt a powerful love for Mimi, that difficult woman,
unfolding her camp bed in the dining room.

As in a fairy tale, the human condition
is always to wish for the wrong thing.

# LIFE ON MARS

When you travel to Mars
it's so boring
you have to take heaps of Tabasco.

You look at the puffy white walls
(they have almost literally
uploaded you to the cloud)

see the same loose wires
the same home planet
stuck on the window like a petal.

If you want to look at a website
you have to put in an order:
good luck with *shemale dormroom*.

They know that when you are bored
you become more racist, less hungry,
more likely to electrocute yourself just for kicks.

So they start to make life more difficult
for your own sake
they make you walk for miles

to collect your bag
and they make you cook
because there's just enough gravity

to keep tomato paste powder in the pot.
You spend more time on variations of lasagne
than exploring lava tubes, but that's ok

that's to be expected.
And the boredom brings on nostalgia
you remember the sound of gulls

how it travelled down your hearing
like a tumbling series of single brackets
fallen on their side

and you remember
how they came to the park
in anticipation of a storm at sea.

# LIGHTNING

Women are less likely to be struck by lightning
for all the boring reasons – we spend less time outdoors
on steppes and plains and open fields
while the sky develops its magnificent headache.

So we must be satisfied with terrors
that are less *august*.
Mopeds in the rear-view
near misses with doors and hinges

the banality of medicine
its bootees and waiting around
and nowadays you walk to the theatre yourself
and climb up onto the table.

# CHERRY BLOSSOM TIME

Pale grey and white seagulls
held up by storm force winds.

This would be cherry blossom time
if there were any cherry trees here
if there were any blossoms.

They say that half the money spent on advertising
is wasted, but no one knows which half.
It's the same with the time spent on the planet.

You find you have irrational fears
or rational ones
the fear that your head
that old, water-damaged clock
is doing bad things to the rest of you.

You look around, even those who are closest
those within your own body
turn out to be living on a different island

here it's just you, your trousers with ragged cuffs
like the teeth of a saw

and your variations on the same old joke
how you put something in a bottle

see something on the horizon
maybe one of those cruise ships

that when they come are bigger than the city.

# THE PARTY

*for Jane and Andrew*

In this city you will always be above and below
so it was at the party

conducted on the deck, as of a ship
while beside at head height

the neighbour's chimney pot turned slowly;
black hat of Renaissance clergyman.

As with the ancient feasts of yore
seafood had been macerated since dawn.

A wide-eyed baby drank from a bottle
while its father held another to the mother's lips.

The older you get, the more worried you appear.
You aren't worried, of course, you're just singing

you're looking over the heads of relaxing strangers
to where the hills are rising up like mountains.

You think a lot about *the highlands* now
they are not a place in Scotland

they are the suburbs you always knew
and now you see how mists and clouds come upon them

and how they rise up from the flat places
against the sky.

Down on the lawn, people were playing badminton
or, playing with badminton equipment.

Garry played a trick for John:
with four shuttlecocks he hit all at once

they flew from the racquet as magician's doves
to the net where they hung, white, in the dusk.

# CIVIL TWILIGHT

The time of night when men
going home to babies
are walking past trees shrieking with birds.

I look out to the water
that piece of the sea we call the harbour
it is pink, or it is grey and damaged looking

and all around the suburbs
rising up. My home town
the place I made almost all of my mistakes.

At the top of concrete stairs
and in showers, seen in mirrors
I did violence to myself through seeming not to care.

I listened to tapes for years
released anger into mountain streams
and took my child self in my arms

she always wore school uniform, though I never had.
So here I am. The streets of the town
go in different directions now

they had to write on the ground *look left, look right.*
And if I say that when I see myself in the window
of the bus I resemble an elephant

I don't mean that unlovingly.
Just that I look surprisingly human
with my long face and my memories.

# WASTER OF THREE BOWLS

*i*

The small figures aren't special.
Cast from moulds, produced in bulk.
Some were gods but some were simply people
a boy with a hat or was it a boy with a harp?
Maybe you just keep him around
to remind you of the countryside.

I recall two precious types of figures from my childhood.
The china dogs that came with toothpaste,
flowing ears and coat, the colour of a brown teapot.
Even then they seemed faintly archaic
like they came from another time
or from England.

And the clear plastic animals.
My favourite was the deer –
its elongated legs and pointed ears tipped with pink
but transparent, as if in a fairy tale
where creatures of the forest
were made of hard sugar.

If my mother were not such an extreme anti
sentimentalist, I might have those figures now.

*ii*

Just recently, mum threw away Oggie Doggie,
left with her for repair.
She didn't recall the Khandallah Fair
circa 1977, how she had increased my spending money

from fifty to seventy cents
to allow the purchase.

I still remember the surge of gratitude
her act of generosity like a kindly monarch
extending to the least of her subjects
a moment of grace. A sense almost of disbelief
that such a thing could come to pass!

But I don't care. Or I write the words I don't care.
If she sweeps away with her hand everything that was:
the monster maze and the painting of Dad
*wearing black nailpolish and eating a liquorice ice cream*
and the pink tipped fragile deer, its black eyes painted on like commas:
She giveth and she taketh away.


*iii*

I am the museum and I am the tomb.
I am the place with the fragments.
I am the waster of three bowls
fused together in an accident in the kiln
and I will tell you everything
everything you can know
about what they call the civilisations of the past
by which they mean, the things
and the people who made them
and the people who kept them
and the people who threw them away.

# AUTUMN, WITH YOUR RARE *MN*

The season comes in
I feel it in the fruit that is no longer adequate

and in the spiders
making their voyages west.

In myself, anonymous pains
give way to known afflictions.

I feel a fleeting passion for my car
its dark blue body

and for countries, there they are
clustered together

on one side of the globe
while on the other there's just lines and numbers.

But I was talking about autumn
the season of bad news.

I returned from a journey full of grapes
real, highly scented grapes

and the sun was low as I drove round the Basin
and you were lying dead

in that part of the green belt where a man,
quite uncannily, practised his trombone on an outcrop.

I only made hot cross buns one year
but I made dozen upon dozen

and set them to rise in the car
which then smelt wonderful for days.

Somehow I am going back
I am wiping clean the benches

of old houses, standing at kitchen windows
with the light falling in on my face

I am my own daughter, my own son
remembering with a shock how beautiful I was

in the sixties, in the eighties, in the thirties and forties
when I lived through all eras of hardship and plenty.

There was only one kind of parsley then
that you would pick for your mother, as little trees.

# THE CATSKILL MOUNTAINS

There is a world of things that bees can see
which we cannot. They sense the earth's
magnetic field, the electricity
driven by the molten core.

I know that in my heart of hearts
I am not someone who loves the country.
But I do crave the idea of it
to fall upon its soils in relief

to live in a cabin, in a hollowed out tree
in the *Catskill Mountains.*
Of course what I really want is America
not the real one, the wide, wide one

with its purple this and that
and the big gold moon trapped in its branches.

# SLEEP IS MONEY

You are reading the biography
of the biography
of Winston Churchill.

I myself am covered in elephants
their soft weight upon me
their mourning, and their memory.

Let's sleep under an ocean – no
let's sleep under space
the weight of all its moons.

Our ancestors aren't watching
they're on the decks of ships
or dressed in heavy gowns of honour.

Futures creep from our bodies
and climb into wooden dinghies.
They find keys on strings connected to corks

dive for treasure
but it gets too cold, too far
and you can only stay a little time

at the point on the lake
where the tower is visible
between two trees.

Anyway, we sleep through all that.
Our anglepoise lamps watch over us
like dark, solicitous flamingos.

# ANTIMONY

Everything that's important now
was here to start off with
we just didn't know it
it was a coral, growing out from a cave
or it was something that marked our hands.

You spend a long time as the boat
the stone, the peripatetic bird
then one day you look around
you are casting a shadow,
you get between the sun and the ground.

When I look out to sea
I feel myself a reckoning point.
Like the woman at the front of a ship
I have everything in front of me
and everything behind me.

# NOTES

32: I acknowledge the Kenneth Koch poem of the same title, 'One Train May Hide Another', in *The Collected Poems of Kenneth Koch* (New York: Alfred A. Knopf, 2005).

72: The final lines of 'Admit one' are borrowed from 'A Byzantine Nobleman in Exile Composing Verses' by C.P. Cavafy, in *C.P. Cavafy: Collected Poems*, translated by Edmund Keeley and Philip Sherrard, edited by George Savidis (Princeton: Princeton University Press, 1992).

99: The italicised sections of 'The mirror of simple annihilated souls' are quoted from *The Mirror of Simple Souls* by Marguerite Porete, translated by Ellen Babinsky (New York: Paulist Press, 1993).

102: In 2006, news wires carried the story of a black swan in north-western Germany which appeared to have fallen in love with a plastic pedal boat in the shape of a white swan.

104: Shan Jordan is the pianist who appears in the poem 'Deep navigation'.

107: With acknowledgement of Czesław Miłosz's poem 'An Alcoholic Enters the Gates of Heaven', in *New and Collected Poems (1931–2001)*, translated by Robert Hass (New York: Ecco, 2003).

109: The world record for the longest bout of hiccups is currently held by Charles Osborne who hiccuped for 68 years, from 1922 to 1990. Osborne said the hiccups started while he was slaughtering a hog.

137: Even before his mother's early death, John Lennon lived much of the time with his Aunt Mimi.

142: The poem 'The party' is dedicated to Jane McKinlay and Andrew Zielinski, whose party it recalls, but more generally to the singing group that I am so glad to be a part of, the Doubtful Sounds. Garry Smith and John Crump, son of Doubtful Sounds maestro Bryan Crump, appear in the poem.

145: 'Waster of three bowls' was written in response to the 2016 exhibition *Inspired: Ceramics and Jewellery Shaped by the Past* at Te Papa. I had not encountered the concept of a 'waster' before – a ceramic piece damaged during manufacture, especially during firing.

# ACKNOWLEDGEMENTS

My publishing career began thanks to the creative writing programme at Victoria University of Wellington, established by Bill Manhire and taught in my year by Damien Wilkins. I am so grateful for that early encouragement.

It is a wonderful thing to have an insightful, honest editor who is also kind; thanks to Fergus Barrowman at Victoria University Press I have enjoyed that luxury throughout my career. Thanks also to Ashleigh Young who has edited this book with meticulous enthusiasm, and to the whole VUP team.

Many of these poems have been written on residencies, including the Katherine Mansfield Menton Fellowship and the Creative New Zealand Berlin Writer's Residency, and during my time as writer in residence at Waikato University. Thanks to Creative New Zealand, the Winn-Manson Menton Trust, the Arts Foundation and Waikato University. Thank you also to the editors of the publications in which some of these poems have previously appeared.

For almost twenty years, my writing group has been integral to my creative process. Workshopping with these wonderful women is a joy and a necessity. Tusiata Avia, Hinemoana Baker, Stefanie Lash, Maria McMillan and Marty Smith: Love you, love your work.

Kevin Connolly's belief in my work was an amazing bolt out of the blue when he was at *Brick*, and again when he moved to House of Anansi Press. I feel so lucky to be publishing with House of Anansi and their talented team. Kevin's incisive and generous interrogation of the poems is what every author hopes for – thank you. Thanks also to Stephanie Burt for her kind words and generosity of spirit.

The love of my family gives me courage and a place of safety. Thank you to my father Michael Camp, my sister Mary Camp, and my mother Elaine Lynskey. Mum's quoting from vast reserves of poetry committed to memory is where this all started.

And to my husband Paul Mulrooney, who makes me happy, though human, every day. Thank you darling.

# INDEX OF FIRST LINES

Grant Maiden

KATE CAMP was born and lives in Wellington, New Zealand. She is the author of six collections of poetry and the recipient of all New Zealand's major literary awards. Camp is also an essayist, a memoirist, and a literary commentator, known for *Kate's Klassics*, a nationally syndicated radio program on classic literature that has been running on Radio New Zealand for twenty years. Camp's work has appeared in many journals at home and internationally, including *Landfall* and *Sport* (New Zealand), *HEAT* (Australia), *Brick* and *Arc Poetry Magazine* (Canada), *Akzente* (Germany), *Qualm* (U.K.), and *Poetry* (U.S.). She works at Te Papa, New Zealand's national museum.